GUARDIANSHIP GULAG:

"The Perfect Crime

By The Color Of The Law"

I0698316

by

Dennis Andrew Ball,

author, TYRANNY FROM THE BENCH

"Fighting & Surviving America's Judicial Nitemare!"

Copyright © 2024 Dennis Andrew Ball

ISBN 13: 9798397207270

<u>DEDICATION</u>

"THIS BOOK IS DEDICATED TO AMERICANS

WHO SACRIFICE EVERYDAY TO PRESERVE

PROTECT & DEFEND OUR LIBERTY &

FREEDOM FOR OUR CHILDREN&

GENERATIONS TO COME!

NOW THE TIME HAS COME FOR A NEW

GENERATION OF AMERICANS TO TAKE THE

REIGNS OF STATE & MAKE THEM WORK AS

THEIR OWN IN THE BEST INTERSTS OF THE

PEOPLE, THEIR CHILDREN, THEIR FAMILIES

AND GENERATIONS TO COME!

TABLE OF CONTENTS

ACKNOWLEDGEMENT

"Justice is Mine thus sayeth God"

Author's Foreword

I am reminded by history past the history of the United States would not be complete if it were not for those gallant men and women who in the face of danger, proceeded to do something Special about it! America's very existence is tied to her people THE PEOPLE since the founding by a Belief in a Supreme Being with an invisible hand guiding the United States of America.

For those who cannot accept this premise, find it within yourselves to exam yourselves in America and the World have continued to show all of us how vulnerable our "Senior Population" is to **Judicial Misconduct, Greed & Theft!**

Author, Dennis Andrew Ball addresses these abuses showing the way out by generations of government entities have allowed to be created including every President since President Kennedy.

He also shows the history of America how through subterfuge and manipulation of her foreign & domestic policies put at risk our very ability to survive and thrive as a people & nation.

Read what must be done to bring America back to herself and her people to protect themselves From GUARDIANSHIP GULAG: THE "Perfect Crime By The Color Of The Law!"

THE PROBLEM

1. GETTING OLD.

The *history of America* would not be complete if it were not for the men and women who sacrificed much of themselves for a new nation and their children. Of course, much can be said of those who plotted against them and used them to profit at their expense. For those they must answer for us we must correct their mistakes for our children and generations to come. This then, becomes the back ground for

GUARDIANSHIP GULAG:

"The Perfect Crime By The Color of The Law"

"You cannot help the poor by destroying the Rich."
"You cannot keep out of trouble by spending more than you earn." "You cannot lift the wage earner by pulling down the wage payer" – Abraham Lincoln

---

"I have always been afraid of banks."

"One man with courage makes a majority" "It is to be regretted that the rich and powerful too often bend the acts of government to their own selfish purposes." "Take time to deliberate but when the time for action arrives, stop thinking and go in." – *Andrew Jackson*

Let it be said, that America's finest hours are yet to come because the Children Of America can make a contribution to not only our Nation but also the World!

We are the product of generations past, present and future with the belief that our rights come from God; NOT THE STATE at a great cost to those who fought and died for them! That was the Social Contract created in 1781 at Yorktown-Gloucester Bay, Virginia.

The monuments laid at the reefs of those so honored are a testament to the sacrifice of so many for the hope that their sacrifice would *bear.* A proud nation was born and with it the greatest nation on earth in the history of man, *"AMERICA!"*

THE NATIONAL BACKGROUND

Early History

What was assumed by those in power was taken for granted by those struggling to live out their dreams. *AMERICA* was a land of opportunity because it's people made it their priority to continue living out their dreams for a better life for themselves and those for their children.

Colonial America grew at an astounding rate by the span of time from the founding of the Republic at Jamestown, Virginia 1607 until the last entry known as Georgia Colony 1732.

Of course, many events in between the time of founding and establishing Colonial life dominated the culture legally and politically;

particularly making it possible for 2.5 million people to realize their value because the Bible was read in the home, the schools and the Supreme Court! Ethics & Morales were also taught in the home practicing honesty and good business including honest services. The attitudes within the culture was fairness as the colonies grew in population and agriculture.

As a result, the *Great Migration* ensued so that by the beginning of the War For Independence, *AMERICA* had enough population to fight England for it. And so we did on July 4, 1776 by way of the Declaration Of Independence, Congress, Philadelphia, Pennsylvania.

Now many of the colonists believed God blessed and reserved America for them to conquer and take dominion ownership of the land being contentious because Wars for land belonging to native populations were in dispute culminating in settlements agreed to by their Chiefs & Council Of Elders.

Fast forward to today's society, there still exists a system based representation of enumeration of census as to the number of folks that occupy individual states. However, the 16th Amendment did away with the census enumeration and went to a direct tax on income which now includes the Standard Deduction and deductions based on gains and losses. This is the problem America is plagued. This impacts young & old alike.

Could it be those with the most to lose tie themselves up with the government for as long necessary to keep themselves from being penalized for surreptitious acts they commit during the period of doing their business?

That is my point, unlike the history of *Early America* when life and government was much simpler and much smaller than now, we Americans did not have to deal with so much regulation & taxation without representation. Executive session was not the experience as it is *today, meaning less transparency.*

And So, since President William Howard Taft, a man who held Office as both President and later as Chief Justice, history records his participation in the events that mark 1913 as a Turning point in American history.

Events do have a way of marking themselves to follow the outcome of what creates tremendous conflicts and tragedy in the lives of our Citizens & our Children.

It is within this context that government *Of, By & For The People* must survive and thrive in this the twenty-first century and beyond because in the nation and world, we are all getting Older.

GUARDIANSHIP GULAG is that vehicle to get us where we can understand what must get done to correct the problems created by our national loss of sovereignty

that can restore our standing in the World and
put an end to the mindless currency
manipulations from European & Domestic
Bankers.

They whom own the Gold controls
the masses. *AMERICA* must take back
her economic sovereignty by correcting
the structural decay allowed to be created in
order to make every other model obsolete in
the process of governing our People and
assisting generations to come.

Getting old triggering predatory
guardianship during the post war years since
1945 is a huge problem today. Both variations
of conservatorship strips a person of their
rights to life, liberty and the pursuit of
happiness. It has turned into a Gulag
separating individuals called "Wards" to a
cottage industry of nursing homes controlling
family members away from their loved ones.

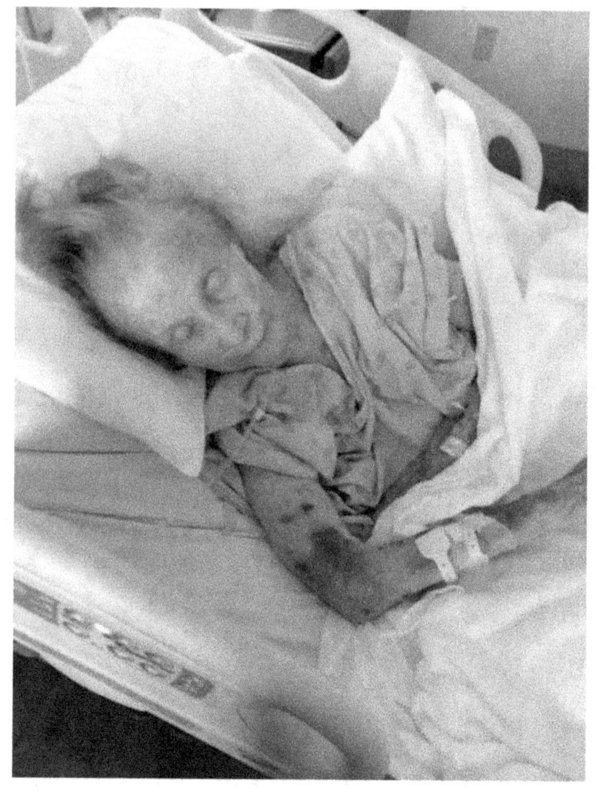

2.$YOUR MONEY$.

Now if it isn't enough getting old, the burden again falls on either ourselves or the family we are born.

And with that the financial support necessary to maintain and sustain the lifestyle we claim.

Stocks, Bonds, $ecurities, Bank Accounts, Certificate of Deposits, Annuities designed to support retirement age less properties, homes and the lifestyle enjoyed during the *Freedom* years.

.   Is America suffering from years of emotional and financial abuse caused by greed and forces conspiring to destroy our nation and make us and our children slaves to the State?

Have we become a nation of indifference personal gain & profit by any means possible?

This is the core of the problem facing the Nation and the World, but that there is a better way for all of us to live, breath & have our being in a society that needs correcting.

<u>MAKING THE CASE</u>

The Bible says "The Love Of Money Is The Root Of Evil" 1Timothy 6:10

But I add that it is also the love to command and control one's life & future.

They who participate in the Gulag know what they are doing to innocent family members, primarily females who are either widows, frail and ill.

Lawyers, Courts filled with family court judges probate court judges raid into the assets of our most vulnerable citizens.

Instead of protection, EXPLOITATION of them, the "Wards" is now the norm in our society.

The love of money has taken over in our midst making jurisprudence non-existent in a Pluralistic society. This then is the problem with no bounds for failure of law enforcement doing their job. As a consequence, 'The People' suffer at the hands of a broken system of theft and injustice with few in law enforcement willing to hold them accountable when in fact it should be the norm.

The problem of the Gulag continues to be peeled away as we look closer into it.

3. GUARDIANSHIP.

What is it?

When we hear the word, many of us including myself, think of a child's life being the focus of an adult having control over the child's life.

However, in the case of Adult guardianship, it is a completely different matter caring for aged parents or spouse who cannot take care of themselves without adult care and supervision. This then is the weakest link by where power and control over vulnerable adults begins abuse in the broken system by design by the Courts.

Both Patrick Henry and George Mason, Founders of the American Revolution, were opposed to the ratification of the American Constitution for fear that those in the Judiciary branch of government would use their power to hide behind it.

They argued that an unbridled judiciary could undo what was fought and died during the revolution. Washington warned at his inaugural address that America could lose if those who sought power by controlling the people, became tyrants by which many died.

Unfortunately, his prophetic voice and that of Abraham Lincoln are being fulfilled. America has become a wasteland and watershed for every tom, dick and harry to use abuse and misuse anybody at anytime with little to no consequence. How long can this go on? The problem is vast and massive with billions of dollars changing hands victims stripped of their rights nursing homes enriched with appointed for profit guardians unquailed to care for their clients.

The Gulag is trafficking victims from families separating drugging liquidating then killing them off. It is no different what Nazi Germany conducted by their extermination camps only this time it is here in America being conducted by the Color of the law.

Once the person's estate is liquidated then its off to the next victim. Law enforcement stays in the shadows allowing for the mass homicide of thousands. It is a holocaust, with the State having blood on their hands. It is a public safety matter.

Guardianship is synonymous with human trafficking creating a Gulag of extermination no accountability calling it a "Civil Matter".

What is truly disturbing is that the Federal government has known for years yet has done nothing to protect society from this abuse. Obviously, Congress sits on their laurels while "The People" suffer.

When in the course of history, the federal govt. fails to act to protect the people from the tyranny of the State, then the people have the right to correct it. How they choose to correct it has many choices all of which goes to the heart of the problem, Accountability.

Change will not come until accountability is restored and reestablished.

The trafficking of American citizens for their money and property by the Color of the law are CRIMES against humanity and as such must be Severely PUNISHED!

4. THE COURTS.

Who Are They? What Are They?

Both State & Federal Courts are here to hear complaints brought by the public from matters they seek a just answer.

That's what they were designed initially to do. However, since the organization and formation of the State Bar Associations, there has been a rapid decline in the number of judgments for the people and an accelerated rapid response for defendants who are sued but file motions to dismiss or found unaccountable by the Bar or the Bench.

Many of these defendants are either corporations or entities working against the interests of the people instead using them to satisfy their own.

Unfortunately, our society has allowed this intrusion into the affairs of the people to the detriment of all.

Examples abound of American citizens kidnapped against their will by a Court Order placing them initially into a temporary Guardianship and then after trial a permanent one.

The victim has been stripped of their Constitutional rights, life liberty pursuit of happiness is gone and living status is reduced to four walls, a bed, and poor nutrition. This is worse than being placed in a cell block with other prisoners, except these folks have done nothing to place them except being rich and old.

This is how the Gulag is sustained by the involuntary incarceration of our family members particularly females who statistically out live their husbands.

1980--79.3 W

1980--73.5 M

WOMEN ARE THE TARGETS OF
THESE LEGAL PREDATORS.

Let me tell you a story when I was much younger naïve and ignorant to the workings of the Court system in the United States.

After graduating from the University Of California San Diego 1973, I embarked what for me I thought would be promising law degree and legal career. What I didn't know was behind the scenes, a cancer was growing on the culture regarding the health and wellbeing of our *Senior* population.

This cancer attached itself on the daily workings of the State Bar Associations by the Color of the law. As a result certain aspects divorce, child support and probate of Wills & Trusts were making their way in front of Court appointed judges adjudicating the future lives of their litigants.

On hearsay alone, many decisions by

these Courts were Unconstitutional and illegal yet they did not care because the lawyers and Court appointed judges were making a good living and lots of money at the expense of their senior victims particularly women.

At 22 years old I withdrew from the Gulag making discovery of other aspects of law enforcement I wanted nothing more to do.

I was not going to humiliate myself at the expense of enriching myself at the expense of servicing the Court.

At 22 years old, I was not going to participate any further in what I perceived then as a corrupt legal system supported by Bankers targeting little old ladies for their money and property when their husband died. Little did I think or know how much

"WE NEED A WINNER BECAUSE THE FEDS DON'T PAY US FOR EQUAL CUSTODY DECISIONS"

worse it would get once I decided lawyering was not for me, since coming from a successful WWII Great Depression era family.

5. THE JUDGES.

Who is responsible for this tyranny on

"We The People?'

The Gulag has had many years to perfect their scam on "We The People" and driven many of them into bankruptcy without any hesitation.

This is pure Evil that has taken root in the culture and the Judges responsible in tandem with the State Bar Associations.

These Judges also preside on the State Supreme Courts supervising their State Bar Association. How convenient is that? Not only do the they get to make the rules, but also to make sure they are enforced!

The Gulag is perfected to cause permanent injury upon those it touches. God help us that society sees it for what it is and decides to Fight for the Right that makes Might!

The Federal government has allowed all of these scams to go unchecked by the three branches of government including law enforcement on the State level including Governors. As a consequence, the Gulag thrives and continues to be a public safety matter.

<u>THE SOLUTION</u>

6. LIEN FILING.

In my book "Tyranny From The Bench", I map out a plan holding these bad actors accountable for their criminal acts.

Using the tools of Justice, I developed a system by which damages by predators are actionable by lien filing of their assets in the County Recorder's office where they reside.

Consequently, those liens stay on the books until satisfaction is realized by me for damages done by them.

In the meantime, complaints need be filed against them for the damages they have done to you. DO NOT IGNORE THAT!

There are three (3) areas of the law that have no statue of limitations regarding damages inflicted upon you. They are:

1. FRAUD ON THE COURT.

2. CONSPIRACY TO DEFRAUD.

3. CONTINUING VIOLATIONS.

All three of these torts require action on our part to bring them to court if they do not choose to settle with you. However, be sure you have the evidence to back your liens and complaints. Otherwise you hold yourself out to prosecution. Make sure you can show your damages and the unlawful acts committed against you and the estate.

1. What is Fraud On The Court?

    Answer: "Deliberate acts to cause injury absent the facts to back it up in Court proceedings before the Bench".

2. What is Conspiracy To Defraud?

    Answer: "The organization of a group

or groups with intent to gain access to

one's assets without legal authority or

legal standing; the result being a

complete wipe out of the person's

estate."

3. What Are Continuing Violations?

Answer: In my case my case began in

2005 and is still going! This is by

design to suck every penny out of you

to enrich a broken court system full of

corrupt officials who defy the

Constitution with the intent to keep

control of your money and property or

what may be left after they have

dissembled them. There is no statue of

limitations on the statue and that all 3 provisions are actionable in a Court of law.

Remember, litigation can be expensive because the system is stalked that way. Fair or not, we must play with a plan to make it work for you. That's knowledge & educating ourselves in the law including case law.

You cannot sit on the sidelines and think you'll win. Communicating, learning and fielding questions that pertain to the facts of your case requires your complete attention.

Without this degree of commitment, success may be doubtful but failure is certain.

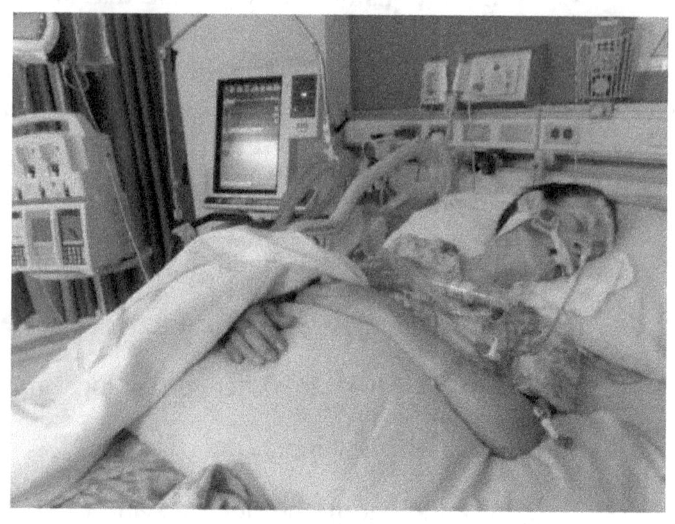

7. IRS FINAL TAX RETURN.

Tax form 3949-A pertains to individuals or companies assigned to the care of persons within their care who are paid by their estates.

This is an important provision within the law to protect tax payer exploitation by criminal means particularly a certain group of vulnerable adults waiting to be extorted for their money on a ruse of care that does not meet a "Standard Of Care".

Without naming names, there are lists of subpar contractors who are recipients of massive complaints only to change their name and continue doing business.

Failure to file a final tax return upon the End of their client's care subjects them to an Investigation into income tax fraud by the Internal Revenue Service including State income tax where applicable.

This is a weapon in the fight for justice that should be explored by filing a complaint upon the entity who has caused much harm.

INTERNAL REVENUE SERVICE FORM 3949-A COMPLAINT AGAINST SUSPECTED TAX

FRAUD BY A FIDUCIARY
ASSIGNED BY COURT ORDER.
****NOTICE: MAKE SURE YOU
FILL OUT EVERY LINE THAT
REQUESTS INFORMATION
ABOUT THE BAD ACTORS WHO
USED YOUR FAMILY TO PROFIT.
THEIR FAILURE TO FILE ESTATE
FINAL TAX RETURN TRIGGERS
YOUR COMPLAINT TO THE IRS.

This is how the notorious Al Capone was taken down by law enforcement which he died in prison.

All those he harmed were restored and their families. Law enforcement has a duty to support citizens who find themselves extorted by criminals including those in the

American Judiciary where ever they may

reside.

8. COLLECTING THE EVIDENCE.

Now that you have filed the liens and possibly a complaint for the guardian's failure to file a final tax return IRS Form 3949-A on their ill gotten gains, it is now time to organize your evidence in a coherent organized fashion to present to the Court in your complaint at the time of filing or upon discovery.

Evidence is key in support of your filing of liens upon the defendants who allowed so much harm to the estate of your loved one or ones including their personal safety at the hands of those who violate their "Standard Of Care."

In my case, I have stacks and boxes of all kinds of filings including exhibits and case law in support of the number of violations these bad actors commit like pigs at a feeding trough.

Interrogatories, depositions, interlocutories are brought to show corroborating support for the evidence you have amassed and/or continuing to amass.

You use this support in creating your Complaint. The complaint is necessary to show the Court what happened and damages that resulted.

Billing receipts, invoices, bank records, Time sheets, correspondence, accounting Book keeping or Forensic audit, ALL are Evidence in support of your case including Activity generated by the Court upon estate Assets, property, rental receipts, trust tax records, collection of rents or failure to collect, pay insurances or failure to pay.

Show the Court with your evidence a Total Collapse of the estate with pigs at the Trough using abusing and liquidating every aspect of their clients portfolio.

This EVIL is not limited to the Court alone but also to those who *crony* with them.

The psychologists who tell the Court, a Guardian is necessary in every case persons brought to them. The scam continues that a family member would be inappropriate for the position because there may be a conflict in the family that is irreconcilable, so we let the Court appoint a for-profit shell company to shake down fleece the family and their loved one or ones.

Then placing their client in a facility foreign to both her/him out of their home, selling off their assets, disrupting their entire life with a Court directed scam using the system to justify their aims with the number of litigants waiting to be exploited is everything they were not designed to do.

For these reasons alone, my withdrawal from becoming a lawyer is/was JUSTIFIED!

Now, as a Court appointed TRUSTEE, my role is not only a litigant as a sole beneficiary but also an appointed prosecutor holding those accountable for the damage done to the estate and mother who's aim of a dysfunctional daughter was to prey on her mother and her estate.

This story can be repeated many times but how to navigate through these perils, and come out on top means "We The People" have been had by an unscrupulous Gang of Court thugs like pigs feeding at the trough of their clients estates or worse liquidating them out right with their bodies reduced to cremation urns stored at lockers in a warehouse or worse their actual place of business.

I hope this scares the dickens out of you to know this may be waiting for your future!

EVIL has come to this generation without our consent or asking. We must Fight, collect the evidence file the Complaints and make our way to Federal District or Bankruptcy Court.

There, they can be heard with the Demands for Jury trials, convictions, Judgments, compensation and damages.

As I have said in other titles, "If your Not Fighting For Your Family, Whom Are Working fore?" This is a key principle of

Life & Longevity. God created the family!
He included it in His Ten Commandments.
"Honor your Father & Mother that you may
Live a long and good life." God knew what
he was doing to protect His people.

Unfortunately, many people do not know
or seek what to do to resolve this conflict in
their lives. Many don't even care what the
consequences are regarding their conduct.

For that they have no one to blame for a
drug addicted life they live unfulfilled &
depressed. The crisis within their souls
is real and causes much anxiety as they
traverse life without God and hope for
a better future.

Some find themselves homeless and
unable to cope with their life's condition.
Some recognize they have options and

pursue them with the support of others.

It is this author's opinion that each of us has an opportunity to discover our destiny by the works we engage. Karma is a real force of life that visits everyone when time and distance shrink.

The Bible speaks of it in several of the Old & New Testaments. There is moral law within *the natural laws* of God for all human behavior to acknowledge and follow; especially as it relates to the wellbeing of the family unit.

Our hope is to learn and grow in "faith" to bring others into the Kingdom of God for all humanity to acknowledge for the benefit of their children and generations to come. This is our ministry to shine the light for all to follow into the Kingdom of God to make a World safe for us and for our children.

The Kingdom Of God is neither a place nor a State of Mind but a Dimension that defies time & space.

Some have described It as being released from the mother's womb into a Universe unlike any other.

9. FILING THE COMPLAINT.

The Gulag is real touching Celebrities, the Rich & Famous, depleting their money, wasting their property, selling their assets making them paupers.

Not only themselves but others who are frugal, saved their money and made their mark. Many citizens find themselves in this middle bracket enough to be preyed upon by the exploiters in the Courts, Bar Members, and Supreme Courts.

These predators associate with each other at their conferences, associations, banquets and believe it or not on the Golf Course!

They all know each other and proceed to cover for one another. Their crimes must be heard and verdicts must be given, "Guilty as Charged!"

Which brings us to the matter of creating the Complaint so it can stick and move forward in the Court.

I have always been a fan of Precis writing, meaning "limited words covering all the aspects of the subject matter at hand." ;compressing words down to their least number to describe the subject matter at hand.

Making your case stick in the Court is your immediate task to keep it from being kicked out. The Judges are good at that so you may want to confer with an attorney prior to your filing or if a Trust is a subject, hire a law firm that is good at restoring it.

You must have evidence to support your Legal claims whether Liens or Claims.

Writing your complaint requires skill

and a familiarity with the law. You may
want to begin the process by engaging in
mock drafts to become familiar with format
how lawyers communicate and use their
skills to advise the parties.

Many of us thought this process would be
quick & easy, it is not. Your evidence must
support your words and the least number
used the better for your outcome. Writing
is a skill, something to be learned with time.

It is unfortunate the system has placed all
of us in jeopardy holding us hostage to the
whims of thugs running it.

This is true in both State & Federal Court.
With your complaint, you will want to attach
a Summons to serve the defendants with you
being the plaintiff.

You will want the Court to certify it and

either hire a process server, Sheriff and/or Marshalls to serve them. In some cases you may be able to serve them by mail with a twenty (20) day response time in certain jurisdictions.

If they fail to respond, you may file for a Default judgment issued by the Court. A hearing may be necessary. You may wish to check with the clerk's office for further details and information.

You can also attach certain documents with the filing of the complaint to show the Court you believe damages are a result.

Those documents can be exhibits to support the Counts you allege happened in the Guardianship including death of the loved one by the negligence of a "Standard Of Care" which is central by the Gulag.

10. GOING TO COURT.

We have covered a lot of ground and I hope your not overwhelmed.

But this is the path of least resistance to Win your case and hold these bad actors accountable.

The cottage industry they created must come down over their heads. As a public safety matter, we all are at risk. We must act making our voices heard. Much abuse of *"We The People"* goes unpunished and with every passing day more people are effected.

The Courts are the 3rd branch of govt. and *Have a duty to serve the people; let justice be done though the heavens fall.*

When you go to Court, file your Complaint have the parties served with Summons. You may wish to hold out an

Olive branch for alternative dispute resolution or ADR sessions be conducted.

Those sessions may turn out to be settlement conferences where major litigation may be avoided.

In that case, you may want to hire counsel to attend with you.

Learn your way by investing your time in proceeding to get educated into the whiles of the Judiciary. They are a Motley bunch. Good luck!